Alvin Jasper was at the top of his country music career. He had everything money could buy but he always felt that something was missing.

Malary was just 16 when she discovered Alvin's music. Through every song he wrote and interview he gave she felt more and more connected to him. She also found her own voice and who she really was. She knew she had to meet him somehow and hopefully tell him how much he means to her.

This is the first book following Alvin and Malary's journey. Kirby Neto is currently working on book two "Catching Blue Marlin" which will be released within the year.

Acknowledgments

I would like to thank my family and friends whom without you my story wouldn't be possible. To my extended family my boating Aunt Patricia Albano for helping me with all the steps I needed to take to make this a reality. You and Butch pushed me to get this story out into the world.

Also a very special dedication to my dad, he always wanted me to do something special with my talents. I hope I made him proud. You may be gone but definitely not forgotten. Now you will be forever immortalized in print.

"In my cowboy days,

They thought it was just a phase,

Now here we are as happy as we can be,

My cowboy and me."

                        Kirby Neto

Cowboy Daze

He was at the top of his career as a country music star. But he felt something was still missing in his life.

She was just a kid when she discovered his music and was overcome with love and admiration with every song he wrote and sang.

Chapter one

The discovery

It was Malary's 16th birthday, her friends and family all gathered around to watch her open her presents. One of her presents was a cassette tape of a country singer she hadn't heard of yet. She was a new country music fan and was excited to get a greatest hits collection from this tall blonde drink of water wearing a cowboy hat with long blonde locks to his shoulders. She thought wow this guy looks so dapper in a maroon suit with a white cowboy hat and black and white snake skin cowboy boots. The bolo tie was officially her new favorite tie now too.

The next day she woke up to her dad playing what would be the start of a whole different life for Malary. It was the voice of Alvin Jasper. He had the type of voice and ability to sing any song and make it sound like the first time you're hearing it. From that moment on she had to know everything about him. So Malary joined his fan club in hopes of getting a bit closer to him and possibly meeting him at one of his concerts one day. Meet and greets were part of the fan club membership!

While waiting for her fan club package to arrive Malary and her mom Josie went shopping for cowboy boots and hat. She also saw a belt buckle she couldn't pass up. She thought she had her birthday money why not spend it wisely? Two weeks after Malary had joined Alvin's fan club she had gotten a package in the mail. It was her official fan club packet filled with a membership card, stats about Alvin, (6'4 from Jupiter, Florida, loves fishing, boats and cars, pretty much anything with a motor. Also, some kind of weird sandwich she just had to try, (well if it was Alvin's favorite it had to b her new favorite too) it also had an 8x10 glossy picture autographed by the one and only Alvin Jasper. The only thing Malary became concerned with was his age. He had just turned 31 two months prior to her 16th birthday in November. Oh well no biggie, she thought, not like she's going to ever end up dating him or anything. Won't stop her from fantasying about it though.

Malary went off to school like she does normally only now she's wearing Alvin Jasper shirts, cowboy boots, and a belt buckle that resembles his. Most kids just look and giggled at her, others talk behind her back and others say mean things about Alvin trying to get a reaction out of Malary. She just carries on ignoring everyone just getting through her day so she can go home and watch his videos and play her guitar to his songs. Just doing what she could to feel closer to him any way possible.

Malary's family was concerned that her love for AJ was an unhealthy obsession and hoped it was just a phase that she'd outgrow in time for college. She only had a couple real friends from elementary school and no one she really called friends in high school yet. Her love for Alvin wasn't hurting anyone though and the by the time she was a senior in high school she overcame her shyness and Malary auditioned to sing one of Alvin's songs at her final senior concert. People started noticing her confidence level growing more and more as she came out of her shell because of AJ's music. She even made some friends before she graduated high school. All of Malary's teachers were so shocked and proud of her for singing at the senior class farewell concert. Some of them even came to root her on during rehearsals. Her family couldn't believe it if they hadn't seen it with their own eyes. Even when they showed the whole family the tape of her singing at her graduation party some family members still couldn't grasp it, rubbing their eyes in shock.

  Her best friends Aggie and Niffer really pushed for Malary to go to college in Tennessee in hopes of getting a chance of bumping into Alvin in town somewhere in or around Nashville. But Malary was afraid to leave everyone and everything behind for what seemed like a pipe dream. Her parents tried to keep her feet on the ground by telling her he has no idea who she was and besides she's too young for him anyway. They're criticism only pushed her to apply for community colleges in Tennessee. She figured while she was in school there she could work and save up for a small place eventually. Aggie said she would join her this way she wouldn't be alone and her parents would feel better knowing that Aggie was there too since she's had Malary's back since they were 4. Niffer couldn't join them only having moved to a new school herself and she just started dating her new boyfriend. Malary couldn't ask her to leave all that behind to support her pipe dream.

Aggie and Malary got into one school together and they were so happy to finally live out a childhood dream of living together, well sort of. One step closer anyway. Aggie also wanted to get a job downtown so they could start saving money for their own place eventually.

Chapter 2

The Move

This was it this was the day of the big move to Nashville. Aggie and Malary were so excited to be on this journey together. It was hard for Malary's parents to send her off to a new state like this though. Malary was sad to leave them but knew it was time for her own life and to pursue her dreams. She had never gone on a trip anywhere without her parents before. She was really close with both of them, so this move is a huge deal for her.

Their parents dropped them off at the airport they said they'd make a trip down there as soon as they were settled in and mail them whatever they needed. The girls promised to call multiple times during the day and text them about everything they were doing. It was the first time Malary had ever seen her dad cry. And that made it so much harder than she ever could have imagined.

It was time to go though so Aggie said, "Don't worry I'm here with you and this is gonna be epic! You'll see your parents soon. You know they can't stand being apart from you for too long." Malary smiled and said,

"That's true, they'll probably be on the next plane out of New England by the time we take off." They both laughed and felt much better about this new chapter of their lives. Besides this is just college it's not like I'm moving away for good or anything, Malary kept telling herself.

The girls got to their dorm and were really shocked at how small it was. They shared a bedroom which was great it was going to be a never-ending sleepover for the year! But they also had to share their common living room with two other girls and a bathroom as well. Both Aggie and Malary were really shy at first, meeting new people in a new setting. But together when they are comfortable they make friends really quickly.

School had started just like any school year had only this time instead of going home to her parents Malary went to a dorm with Aggie and two strangers. It was tough for Aggie to fit in with these girls at first. She's highly protective of Malary and has been since they were in kindergarten. She could tell they were snickering about the Alvin Jasper poster in their room and talks of them joking about cutting class and stocking him one day. They told Malary and Aggie that not everyone in Nashville likes country music and they couldn't wait to get away from it after they graduated.

Malary was use to this behavior from students back home and all through high school but thought that since he does live outside of Nashville people here would be more receptive to her feelings about him. Her and Aggie wondered why anyone would want to move away from Nashville when everything they love is right here.

   For the most part Malary and Aggie only hung out together after that ordeal. They had separate classes and different majors. Aggie was a drama student and Malary was an Art major. They didn't really hangout with anyone else even though they had made friends in their classes. Malary's parents came down once a month to see them and the girls are spending the holidays back home in New England.

   Malary was surprised at how homesick she was once she got back to her old room and spent dinners with her parents talking and laughing at the dinner table like they use to do. She had missed her dog Tiny, their Great Dane, terribly too. Jaycee got him right before she started high school. His previous owners had clipped his ears then didn't like the way he looked so they gave him up. Jaycee knew how mush Malary loves dogs and she always wanted a great dane, plus she'd always have him to come home to. She missed how she would go on walks with Tiny and people passing by would say, "Such a big dog for such a small girl." Malary loved having such a big dog and loved the irony of his name and how she's always the shortest girl in her classes and out of her friends but she has the biggest dog in the group. Aggie had big dogs too her parents had Saint Bernard's and Newfoundland's but Aggie's dog was her Basset Hound Casey. Niffer's mom had a Black Lab and her dad had Vizslas but Niffer had a cat, Blizzard.

Aggie and Malary got through their first year though tougher than they thought it was going to be but they did it. They spent the majority of their summer back home in New England on Malary's parents' boat but wanted to take in some summer fun of Nashville before school started back up again. The girls stayed at a hotel with their parents for a week before they had to go back to school. Malary and her dad, Jaycee, had wanted to ride some horses while her mom went off with Aggie and her parents to go shopping. Malary's mom, Josie isn't one for all this country type living so they hit the mall instead. Besides this gave Malary some much needed father daughter bonding time she had been craving for all year long.

He began to see that his daughter fit right in here and was so proud she had chased her dreams and they were all there together. The only thing missing for Jaycee was the ocean. Malary did miss boating but they do have the Cumberland River and lakes to explore if they ever get a chance to go boating there. Maybe next year they could rent a boat for a day here and there. But nothing beats that salty air!

The girls started their sophomore year this time they had the whole dorm to themselves! Yes! This made it a little easier for them to concentrate on why they were here in the first place, country music and Alvin Jasper of course. Oh, yea and keeping their grades up. Can't forget they're still in school and if she wanted to work for Alvin one day, she really had to have good credentials. Malary isn't an A student so she really needs to put her all in something to achieve the results she's happy with. Keeping her eye on her goals helps keep her motivated and focused in her school work.

Chapter 3

The Moment

   The school year started a little easier for Malary and Aggie this time around. They had a couple of classes together so that helped when it came to homework and studying. They also know where everything is now, not fumbling around like they did last year when they were freshmen. Also not having people make fun of every conversation you have is a plus too.

   One Tuesday morning everything was going on as normal. The girls went to their first classes of the day. Aggie had English class and Malary had science. Everything carried on as usual until they heard something outside in front of the school that sounded like gun shots. Malary was outside in the back of the school during a science lesson. Her science teacher played it off as a car backfiring and everyone proceeded inside to find out it was indeed gun shots.

   Everyone took shelter in either the gym or in the basement where the counselors offices were. That's where Aggie and Malary decided to hide out. Their counselor Mr. Bryan let students hide out in his office and talk or not talk about how they felt about what had just happened.

There was an assembly about an hour later. Everyone was counted for except the disgruntled student that was firing his shotgun in the air to make some sort point. Students were not sent home since no one got hurt. The teachers encouraged students to stay for the rest of the day in hopes they would feel safe enough to return. The gunman was later expelled but everyone was still shaken up including Malary and Aggie.

The next day the girls went to their counselor's office and explained how they felt about coming back to school and expressed their concerns about the people not wanting to come back because of fear of a retaliation. Their counselor Mr. Bryan said he's glad they came back and that they expressed their feelings to him. He told them the school had a plan to get everyone excited to come back to school again. Mr. Bryan said "Just wait and sit tight and listen for news of a rally with a special guest." They left his office and for the rest of the day kept trying to think of who it could be to be coming to the rally.

When word got out about the rally and a surprise special guest that won't be announced until they hit the stage, everyone wanted to come. Malary's parents came and Aggie's too, they even brought Niffer down with them too! They thought no matter who it was, everyone was forgetting about the incident already, so that was a plus. The rally was all anybody could talk about for weeks leading up to it. Excitement filled the halls in a good way again.

  The three girls went with Malary's parents to find their seats and with Aggie's parents too so they could all find seats together. Mr. Bryan came over, looked like he had been out of breath. He introduced himself to Malary's and to Aggie's parents and said he had been looking all over for Malary. He said that the special guest wanted to talk to a student about what had happened and how they had felt about it and he immediately thought of her! Malary was overcome with nerves. She had never met anyone famous before. If the special guest was even famous, they hadn't heard anything about this person just that they wanted to help the school and the students to return to normalcy and in no fear. She thought of that day she and Aggie had gone to Mr. Bryan to talk about their feelings and maybe that's why he had chosen her.

  Mr. Bryan led the way to the security guard blocking the door of what appeared to be a tour bus but there wasn't any name or anything on the bus so she still had no clue who was behind that door. As Mr. Bryan explained who they were and why they were there all Malary could hear was the sound of her heart beating out of her chest. She felt like she was about to pass out or throw up all at once and she had no idea who she was about to meet when all of a sudden, the door opened and who was standing there but the one and only Alvin Jasper!

Her jaw dropped and he said "Hello there darlin, I'm Alvin Jasper. Nice to meet you. What's your name?" In his soft southern drawl and the way, he looked at her she almost didn't realize his hand had been there waiting for hers to shake. She quickly shook his hand and stuttering "I'm...you're, ...how?" Alvin and Mr. Bryan giggled and Mr. Bryan said, "Well Malary my work here is done. You two talk and Alvin, break a leg!"

Alvin sat down and asked Malary to take a seat as well. She sat on the couch across from him sitting at his table. They made small talk that lead to talking about boating and horses and cars and Alvin quickly found out they had had a lot in common. Time was getting closer to show time. Alvin leaned into Malary putting his hand on her knee and asked, "You wanna watch the show from the best seats in the house?" She said, "Of course! I'd love to. But can my friends join me too?" He said, "Of course! Bring your friends and family and whoever else you want! Y'all can stay with my folks in my family section of the stage!" The girls ended up going to the stage and Josie and Jaycee stayed in their seats with Aggie's parents. Malary was on cloud nine watching AJ do his thing on stage and enjoying her VIP treatment.

Chapter 4

The Dream

Malary was still reeling after the rally even weeks later. Her and Aggie finally got to meet and hangout with Alvin. They had completely forgotten what the rally was for in the first place. They were with Alvin every chance they got. When he wasn't out of town performing, he was with the girls. They'd go fishing and boating doing water sports. Alvin really wanted to teach them how to water ski! But that will have to wait until next year. It was already starting to get too chilly to do much on the water other than go fishing and going on day trips.

A few weeks before Christmas break the girls were packing and studying for finals when Malary got a call from Alvin's fan club. She thought, this is weird, why are they calling me I didn't order anything, that I know of. She answered the phone and the president of the fan club was on the other line. She said she was sitting there with Alvin and he had an idea. He remembered that she was in school for art and she was an amazing artist, after all he had signed every painting of him, she had ever done for the last four years! They said they want her to work in merchandising, she'd be designing and thinking up new ideas and designs for all his merchandise. She then put the phone on speaker so Aggie could hear and witness this to make sure she wasn't dreaming. Aggie spoke into the phone and said, "If you have Alvin there with you now put him on the phone so we know this is for real." Alvin laughed and said, "Howdy Aggie this is me it's for real I want her to work with me. I know you girls have school break soon so this is a perfect time to think it over and discuss it with your family. I'm looking forward to working with you." The girls had been holding their breath until AJ finished his sentence and Malary said, "I'm looking forward to it too. This would be a dream come true. And the whole reason we moved here and going to school for!" Alvin said he was so happy to hear that and told the girls to have an awesome vacation and stay safe and he'd see them when they got back to Nashville.

  Malary was so excited to tell her family the news of working for Alvin but when she told everyone on Christmas at her house when all her family was there some of them had reservations about her working for him. They were concerned that it would take away from her school work and she'd lose focus on her career and was this going to be her career? "You have to see if they even like your ideas and designs in the first place" her aunt said. Her uncle said, "Don't skimp out on school because he's a celebrity, he can wait, an education can't and if he can't respect that then he's not in your corner." She had assured them that he had told her the same thing, school comes first. He had quit college after two years to follow a love interest that didn't work out so he didn't want her to make the same mistake. Not that he's a love interest but he was a love interest, she thought to herself. But she wasn't fooling anyone everyone she knew from family to school since she was 16 knew that she was in love with the man. It was hard not to. That soothing voice and long blonde locks. Tall lanky drink of water with a charming southern accent and mustache like Tom Selleck and sex appeal like Sam Elliot. He was the definition of a southern gentleman with a wrangler butt to boot, and could look into those ocean blue eyes for days. But yea no, definitely not a love interest. They're just friends. At least that's what she kept telling herself. She just loved the way he looked at her. His eyes lit up his whole face, he had very expressive eyes. She didn't want to ruin that.

  Malary was so eager to go back to Nashville and tell Alvin what her decision was but he beat her to it. She got a call from him Christmas night, after her family left and she was upstairs in her room relaxing from the holiday. The phone rang and it was a Nashville number so she answered it thinking it was school related but it was Alvin. "Hey there sweetie" he said "I just wanted to wish you a Merry Christmas, how was your day?" Malary was so happy and excited and said, "Hi! Merry Christmas to you too! My day was good. I told my family about working for your fan club they said I should stick to school first then find my career." And rolled her eyes. He said "I understand. You're a sophomore, right? So, you wanna wait two more years then come work with me?" She quickly replied back with a "Hell no! I've waited so long for you to notice me I'm not gonna put a pause on that now!" He giggles and said "Honey I could never forget about you now. Keep talking with your family about it and let me know your decision when you get back. Nothing will change on my end if you want to wait until you graduate. That's important to me too." She so loved this man! "Ok I'll give it some serious thought and I'll let you know. "Alvin said, "Good we'll talk again soon have a good night and sweet dreams love." She was blushing over the phone and smiling ear to ear, "Good night you and sweet dreams, can't wait to see you again." He said, "Me too, bye for now." And they both hung up. All she could think was how can she fall asleep now?!! She thought I have to call Aggie!

Chapter 5

The Friendship

    Malary heard from Alvin again on New Year's, he called her at midnight and said he wanted to be the last one to talk her for the year and the first one to talk to her in the new year. He wished he could be there with her but he had some obligations he needed to be with his family in Florida for the holidays. He's such a mama's boy the youngest of 5, 4 girls and then him. Malary just loved everything about him. But she knew this was only a friendship and nothing more could come from it. He was famous and only dates famous people because that's who his manager and publicist set him up with. Everything he does is strategically planned out.

    When Aggie and Malary got back to Nashville Alvin was waiting for them at the airport, jus him in his ford pickup. No fancy limo or pimped up ride, just him and his truck. Malary ran to him and hugged him, he lifted her off the ground and put her back down. She said, "What a great surprise! This is so much better than a cab!" They all laughed and he said, "Well I hope so! I wanted to see you right away I couldn't wait anymore." Aggie said, "That's so sweet! Me too, right?" She paused and said, "Joking obviously!" He said, "Yea of course you too. I need to hear everything the two of you have been up to." They all talked on the way to the dorm. Alvin helped them bring their bags inside and made sure they were all set he said he'd ask them out for supper but they probably should get settled in and ready for the first day back after vacation. They so desperately wanted to go with him but said he was right; they should unpack and get ready for school the next day. He promised to take them both out another night.

Alvin never broke a promise to Malary he took them out every chance he could. Aggie could see how much he cared for her best friend and she liked him more and more every time they all hung out. She wished she could get these two alone but at the same time loved being included and involved in their friendship. Mostly seeing how happy her best friend was around Alvin and she wasn't shy at all and was completely herself around him.

Malary told Alvin she had thought about the offer some more and took her family's concern into consideration. She said maybe it would be best to wait for the summer to start working for him and then next year work part time while she's in school. Of course, he agreed to whatever she decided to do.

As the weather got warmer Alvin invited the girls to do more and more things with him and sometimes his band as well. He enjoyed taking his band out on his boat and going fishing and waterskiing. Malary and Aggie loved fishing but they left the waterskiing to the boys. It was fun to watch them all and just being with Alvin was enough for Malary. The best nights were the ones where Alvin would cook whatever he had caught and they'd eat on the boat watching the sunset and singing along to the music he played on his guitar.

  Alvin's band the Marlfins could see the two getting cozier and cozier and they voiced their concerns to him but he didn't care. He loved being with her just as much as she loved being with him. Besides nothing was going on between them they were just having innocent fun and getting to know each other. All Alvin knew was he felt whole around her and that was enough for him. He liked not knowing where this was going. Nothing was planned out for him for a change, this was real.

  As summer approached so did Fan Fair. In Nashville the first week of June is nothing but free concerts and meet and greets with your favorite country music stars. Aggie and Malary had always wanted to go but they either had school or couldn't afford it. Even being in Nashville last year they had finals and didn't have the money anyway, but they also didn't know a famous country music star before either. The girls thought of asking Alvin for tickets but didn't because they didn't want him to start to think they're mooching off him because he's famous. They didn't want to chance ruining their friendship with him and the ones made with his band also. So, they went on and studied for their finals. When it got closer Malary told Alvin to have fun and she understands if they can't hangout that week. He said, "Do you really think I'm gonna let you sit at home while I'm signing autographs and singing? I'm not gonna let my best girl miss a second of this Fan Fair. Well at least when you're not in classes." She was so elated after school she met up with him at his bus and he took her everywhere he went. Malary and Aggie stayed with him all day one day watching him interact with his fans and take pictures and sign whatever they wanted him to sign. Then that weekend he put on a free concert and the girls sat at the side of the stage like had at the rally where they all met just at the beginning of the school year. Malary couldn't help but think of how far her and Alvin's friendship had come in just a few months.

  That summer she stayed in Nashville and Niffer came down as much as she could too. Alvin had set up a place for the girls to stay as long as they wanted so they no longer had to worry about dorms or hotels or anything considering money anymore. Malary had told him she always talked about getting a small place near or on a lake where they could have a dock and a small boat. Somewhere family and friends could stay also and maybe ride horses to. He said their families and friends can come and go as they please as well. She was so happy that even if this wasn't going to be anything romantic, she didn't care. He treated her like a queen and her parents knew she was safe with him too and that made her feel even better. As long as this friendship doesn't cross the line there won't be any drama or heartache.

Chapter 6

The Heartache

Word was starting to get around that Alvin Jasper was seen canoodling in public with a much younger woman than him. His name was all over the tabloids as a cradle robber. Malary didn't pay any mind to it they knew their relationship was innocent. Alvin's manager and publicist on the other hand they had other thoughts. They sat down with Alvin and tried to wrap their heads around him setting up a tiny lake house for two college girls who he wants one of them to work for him and supposedly he had no other agenda. He assured them they were not romantically involved and they were just becoming good friends. He explained how she made him feel and that he wasn't just a celebrity to him. "She actually cares for me and I do for her. It's nothing more than that," Alvin pleaded. They could see the look on his face when he talked about Malary.

His manager and publicist told him he can't have any contact with them in public whatsoever. This was bad publicity and his wholesome image would be ruined. Alvin said that's out of the question he wouldn't do that to Malary. They told him there was an award show coming up and he was going to be seen with a famous model his own age and they were going to pose and act like a couple. Alvin was pissed but he agreed to the award show and said after this no more set ups. He just wanted to get out of there as soon as he could to call Malary.

  When Alvin left the office, he noticed his phone was missing he had gone back to get it and his manager gave it back to him said it was on his chair. Must have fallen out of his pocket. He said, "Thanks." And took off. He wanted to go home and call Malary and tell her what jerks they were and that they didn't want him seeing her again but when he got home her number was erased. He couldn't find it anywhere. He had never had to dial it because they're cell phones it was already programmed. He tried looking her up in the fan club archives but he didn't know her home address in New England. Now he's really pissed. His manager must have erased her contact info and is making it impossible for him to get in touch with her. Alvin could still see her at the lake house though! Only it was getting closer to the awards so he had to get fitted for a new suit and boots and hat and coordinate with his date. He wished he could at least give Malary a heads up about all this but school was starting up again too and he didn't want to disrupt her getting ready for that.

  It had been a couple weeks and nothing from Alvin. Malary was starting to worry. She knew the awards were coming on soon so maybe if she saw him perform at least she'd know he was ok and probably just busy. He'd call her again after all this tabloid stuff died down, and the award show frenzy, she hoped.

Her and Aggie turned the tv on to watch the award show. They watched the red carpet like they always do to see the couples arriving and maybe Malary would see AJ. The announcers kept saying they were going to talk to Alvin after a commercial break. Then it was waiting commercial break after commercial break until they said they were set up to talk with Alvin Jasper and see what he's been up to but he was running late and hopefully they'd catch him before the show started.

No luck Alvin hadn't showed up yet. The show started and Malary kept her eyes on the crowd to see if she could see him sitting down. No AJ, but the show had just started he's probably running fashionably late. Of course, they had to wait til the end of the show to see Alvin perform his latest song. They announced he would be after the commercial break and showed him standing backstage with a beautiful blonde woman they had never seen before. Malary's heart sank. Aggie said "Maybe it's just a random chick doesn't mean she's there with him." Malary tried to relax her heart rate and said, "Yea that's true, he probably doesn't even know her." The commercial break was over and he sang and the girls were dancing and singing and they completely forgot about the mystery blonde woman. After he sang there was still a couple awards to give away. This time Alvin was in the front row sitting by the same blonde woman. Malary convinced herself she was a seat filler and Alvin had gone solo to the show. Entertainer of The Year was the last award to give out and Alvin was nominated and what do you know the Entertainer of The Year is Alvin Jasper! As he got up to receive his award his date had grabbed his face and kissed his cheeck. Malary was crushed. She couldn't even hear his acceptance speech. She thought he had met someone new and was done being her friend and all hopes of them being a couple was gone. What she would give to able to kiss him like that.

Another few weeks went by without anything from Alvin. Weeks turned into a month and before she knew it his birthday was coming up. So Malary did what she always did wrote a letter to him through the fan club. She explained she saw the award show and understood if he was busy with his new girlfriend. She said she hoped they could still hangout sometime like they had been doing but understands if he can't anymore. She ended the letter as she always did, "Love you always, Malary."

The day she sent out his letter Alvin's name was in the news, not for his award or new single but his "date" was spilling the beans every chance she could. She said he was a fake and a fraud. They paid her to go out with him and he was a dud of a date. That he didn't even say a word to her the entire time. She was demanding her money back and she was gonna make him pay. Malary started to shake. "Oh no! Alvin must be so embarrassed. That's why he hasn't contacted me!" Aggie said, "That bitch! Who does she think she is talking about our friend like that?! She doesn't even know him. He's not a dud, he probably didn't say anything to her so she wouldn't twist his words around." Malary decided she was going to wait it out and let everything calm down. Every time she tried to call Alvin, she could never get him on the phone. It either went to voicemail or his mailbox was full or got an error message. She thought if he wants to talk to me again, he knows where to find me. Then November came and all she got was an 8x10 of him from the fan club saying he got her letter and thank you for wishing him a happy birthday. Nothing from him for her birthday. Now Malary was really starting to feel down.

  Aggie and Malary were starting to get ready to head home for the holidays once again when Malary got a call but it was from a Florida number. She answered it thinking it was Alvin but it was his mom. She said, "Hi darlin' is this Malary?" Malary said, "Yes, it is." His Mama said, "Hi honey I finally found you. This is Alvin's Mama Jean. Honey you've got to come to see my son he's hurtin' real bad and needs to see you." Malary said, "Of course! Is he home here or in Florida?" Mama Jean said, "Oh no honey he's in the hospital." Malary turned white and said send me the address and room number I'll be right there."

  Aggie drove her to the hospital to see Alvin knowing Malary would be too nervous to drive. When they got there Malary ran in she had to see if he was ok. She found him in his room in the bed. Poor guy looked like he hadn't eaten or showered or shaved all this time. Malary took his hand and said, "I'm here." Alvin opened his eyes and saw her smiling at him and he couldn't help but sob. He covered his face with both hands, just sitting there crying hiding his face. Malary tried to console him but he told her not to look at him or touch him. He hadn't showered in months and couldn't bring himself to eat much. He had missed her terribly and his manager and publicist ruined his life he wanted to crawl up in a ball and just disappear. Malary said, "Alvin Jasper don't you do that to me! I love you too much for you to give up like this." Alvin smirked and said, "Love? You love me?" She said, "Obviously." Alvin laughed and his stomach hurt from laughing but gurgled for the first time in months. He actually asked for his nasty sandwich that Malary had grown to love. She said, "I'll go get you a ham and cheese sandwich with a slice of pineapple in it with a side of ketchup." Alvin grabbed her arm and said, "I love you too." He closed his eyes and slept until Malary came back with food which he ate and then he wanted ice cream for dessert with some pie. He assured her he'd get his strength back and he'd shave and shower so he doesn't look like a homeless person the next time she sees him. Malary leaned in to kiss him but he backed away and said, "I'm so gross looking and haven't showered or shaved in weeks." Malary said, "You could never be gross to me." And she kissed his forehead and he closed eyes.

Chapter 7

The Romance

Malary is home in New England for the holiday break and Alvin was home in Florida with his family resting and getting back to his normal self. It was the day after Christmas and Malary found it odd Alvin hadn't called her to wish her a Merry Christmas yet. She tried calling him but his phone went to straight to voicemail. She had a flashback to the days where his old manager and publicist cut them off of each other. Malary was about to give up on calling him when her dad called her downstairs. He said there's a young man at the door asking for her. She thought that was weird and ran to the door to see who it was. It was Alvin standing in the doorway with a ball cap on freshly shaven, his hair trimmed and neatly brushed to his shoulders. He was wearing a brown leather jacket on top of a jean jacket with a grey sweatshirt under the two jackets. His jeans a bit looser now and a pair of white Reeboks' that looked brand new. She ran to him and jumped up into his arms. He hugged her while her whole body was wrapped around his. Jaycee said, "I guess you know who this is?" He didn't recognize him without his mustache and in all the warm attire, plus the baseball cap threw him off and he was a little thinner now. Malary said, "Dad it's Alvin!

You didn't know it was him?" He said, "Oh he looks like he's 16 or 18 without the mustache! And I guess I'm used to seeing him in warmer weather too!" Alvin said to Jaycee, "Man, you've even got a nice dark tan in the winter!" They all laughed and Josie invited him in. "Take everything off and relax! Well not everything... oh you know what I mean. I'll make some food." Alvin laughed and said, "Thank you. I will just put my jackets over here." Malary took them off the chair that was at the table and put them in the closet and said, "Stay awhile!" With a huge smile on her face.

They all ate delicious Portuguese food cooked by Josie and talked, later on her parents got ready for bed and they asked Alvin where he was staying. He said he'd stay at a hotel for a couple of weeks. He wanted to spend New Year's with Malary and he'd like to go back to Nashville together. They invited him to stay with them instead. Malary had a futon in her room he could sleep on. Malary shrugged and looked at Alvin as if to say you don't have to but of course he took the invitation. He'd been apart from her for too long.

That night they were getting ready to go to sleep. Malary in her bed facing Alvin on the futon and she said, "I have to ask you something I've been wondering all day." Alvin said, "Shoot. Ask me anything." She said, "Why did you shave your mustache off?" He chuckled and said, "It makes me look older and I wanna be with you without people thinking it's creepy." Malary sat next to him and took his face in her hands and said, "I love this face no matter what. I've just always known you with a mustache and thought, wow he looks like a true southern gentleman." Alvin took her hand and asked her, "So what do I look like now?" She said, "A paperboy." They both laughed and got in their own sleeping headquarters, said good night to each other and fell asleep. They woke up a couple hours later to what they thought was the other one snoring away. Then they looked at each other and looked around the room. It was Tiny laying on his back in the hallway to her room. They both laughed into their pillows so they didn't wake him and they fell back asleep. Alvin loved how Jaycee and Josie welcomed him in so quickly.

The next day Malary drove Alvin all around town to show him where she grew up. Her first house, schools she went to and drove by Aggie's house to surprise her. She wished she could take Alvin to visit Niffer but she moved about 2 and a half hours north of them near Vermont. She took him by all the backroads and through the country. Alvin liked the ride back to Malary's parents house through Padanaram Village and over the bridge back to the beach. It reminded him of home just covered in snow and freezing.

He loved spending time with Malary and her family. They always made him feel welcome and he felt right at home there. He loved how Jaycee shook his hand and was always watching him as if to say, I like you but I've got my eye on you with my little girl. Alvin could see where Malary gets her sense of humor from. Her dad has a dry sense of humor and her mom has a nervous sense of humor that makes her say the silliest things. Malary also had her mom's laugh and her dad's smile that lights up her whole face.

It was time to get back to reality in Nashville for the both of them though. But the two of them looked forward to going back together. Before they left together Alvin wanted to sit with Jaycee. He took Malary's dad aside and said, "I think it's pretty obvious I'm in love with your daughter. I want you to know she's safe with me and I'll never hurt her. I only want what's best for her and to see her happy." Jaycee said, "Yes, it is pretty obvious. Thank you for acknowledging it to me though, I respect that. As long as she's safe and happy that's all I care about. But if you ever hurt her, I will have to kill you." He said sarcastically. Alvin said, "I know I'll be swimmin' with the fishes." Jaycee said, "Exactly." Jaycee also appreciated Alvin's sense of humor. They both share a dry wit. Jaycee shook Alvin's hand and winked at him Alvin smirked and went to Malary.

  Alvin and Malary got in Alvin's Private jet back to Nashville. He dropped her off at the house her and Aggie shared, helped her with her bags then he gently tucked her hair behind one ear and held her face as they shared their first kiss. He said, "I wish I didn't have to say goodbye just yet. Then Aggie opened the door and asked if Alvin was going to stay longer. He said he didn't want to over stay his welcome and that the girls should catch up. He'd see them again on New Year's and they'd all ring in the new year together.

  Malary felt so good about finishing this school year. She had Aggie and her man Alvin in her corner to succeed so she can move onto her junior then senior year then finally be where she wants to be career wise and romance wise. Her and Alvin made a deal that they wouldn't get too serious until she graduated.

Chapter 8

The Summer of Love

It was finally summertime. Malary and Alvin had so many plans to be with family and each other until her junior year started. The first part of the summer they went to New England. Malary's parents had a boat and she always wanted to show Alvin around their usual boating spots. She couldn't wait to show him off to all her marina family too. She knew he would fit right in since they already knew everything about him anyway.

First, they went to The Vineyard. Malary's parents always grabbed the same mooring if they could and they'd use a dingy to get to town. Jaycee and Josie thought Oak Bluffs would be a good place to start Alvin off with. It was great he knew how to blend in with crowds so no one could stop him and ask for a picture or autograph. Not that he minded it but he liked to feel like a regular guy too and enjoy his company and vacation.

Alvin loved all the quality time they spent with Malary's parents there and that part of the island. They loved eating at Jimmy Seas then getting pastries at Back Door Donuts for dessert. Or just walking around taking in the sites and shopping during the day then getting ice cream and chocolate at Ben and Bills.

During the week they got together with Aggie and would go out to eat or get ice cream at Salvador's. Horseback riding on the trails and walking Tiny was always a favorite activity. Alvin would take Malary fishing off the dock at the marina because Jaycee was very particular about getting his boat dirty. No fishing off his boat. There's no amount of Windex to clean up that mess!

The following weekend they took Alvin to Eel pond and have the most amazing Swordfish to eat and Lobster Rolls. The best part for Malary was walking hand in hand with Alvin. They felt she felt with her hand in his was like they were the only two people walking on the sidewalk. The next weekend they took him to Vineyard Haven at the Black Dog Tavern. The weekend after that was New Port for the Fourth Of July and they'd watch the boat parade all decorated with red, white and blue and singing patriotic music. That night they went out on the dingy to get a clear shot of the fireworks over the water. The beaches were crowded with people having their own fun with fire pits and dancing around. It was fun to drive by everyone in the dingy just taking everything in.

This weekend was Lagoon Pond just a quiet spot in Vineyard Haven on a mooring. No one else around them. They cooked on the boat and jumped in the water to cool off and swim whenever they wanted. And the dingy races were the best. So much fun when their boating friends would raft up to them too. Then the end of July was Niffer's birthday so they stayed long enough to enjoy to take her out to eat at Sail Loft (everyone's favorite restaurant)

The sunset over the harbor looked extra beautiful that night. Alvin held Malary a little tighter while they looked at the sunset. They walked over the bridge holding hands and talking. They walked to Malary's truck and sat in the truck bed cuddling under a blanket looking at the stars. Something about that night just felt right. That was the first time they made love. It was scary at first but Alvin held her tightly and was a perfect gentleman. He kept asking her if she was comfortable and if everything he was doing was ok with her. She didn't want that night to end. But they had to get back to the house no matter how badly they wanted to wake up in each other's arms.

Malary wished he could experience Block Island with them this summer for Labor Day weekend where they decorated for Halloween then Christmas then new year. Alvin did have to fit in some concert dates as well. They try to work around his boating schedule but it gets tough for them to get enough money for everyone involved to keep them financially stable with very few shows lined up for him. So, he tries to get concerts lined up during the week in the summer time. Mostly Thursday and Friday nights. He doesn't like anyone to complain or go without.

Alvin's new manager set up a big double headliner tour with an up and coming singer, Katharine Amanda

Driscoll. And with a new tour comes new merchandise and new promotional gimmicks and new publicity. Only this tour was a European tour and it was going to take up most Alvin's time.

  Malary was super bummed about not being able to spend the rest of her summer with Alvin. Especially knowing that the tour was going to be in Europe and it would be harder for them to make plans to talk to each other never mind see each other. She knew their love was strong though and she didn't doubt for a second that nothing could break them apart. They hugged each other twice and longer and tighter the second time. They kissed and he took off to the airport promising to keep in touch every step of the way.

Chapter 9

The Split

    Alvin had kept his promise to Malary. He told her everything he was doing. From when he got to London then he was going to his hotel. At the hotel he called her and wished her sweet dreams and told her how much he missed her already. She couldn't believe they were going to apart for so long only having begun they're relationship. He said he loved her and said good night. They hung up their phones but it was still early for Malary she was also going to have to get use to the 7-hour difference. It had been 11:00pm where Alvin is and only 4:00pm for Malary.

    Niffer decided to pay the girls a visit the next day in hopes of getting Malary's mind off of everything. Josie decided to take the girls for lunch then the beach. They met up with a couple of Malary's cousins there as well. It was the perfect distraction. While at the beach someone had mentioned a movie was going to be doing a beach scene there in a couple days. Aggie and Niffer thought that would be the perfect distraction for Malary. They encouraged her to become an extra and they would try to get in too. She reluctantly agreed and they all went to sign up to be extras.

Niffer read up on tips what they look for and what's not accepted for extras. She wanted them all to be a part of it so they could keep an eye on Malary. Luckily, they all made it in. The next day they would film with the actor Dylan Crane, Malary's favorite actor! No way! Now she was getting excited. Niffer was so happy it was someone she liked maybe this would help her forget that Alvin is so far away even if it's for a couple of days.

Word got around that it wasn't fair a famous country singer's girlfriend was going to be in the movie and taking up a spot someone else could fill if she's going to be noticed she could take away from Dylan in the shot. So, they contacted Malary and said she could still be an extra but she couldn't be in any scenes with Dylan so she was crushed once again. Niffer was determined to make it up to her though, her and Aggie just had to get Dylan to meet her just a quick picture and autograph they needed to cheer their best friend up.

They started making small talk around the director and producers saying, "I can't believe we came so close to getting Malary a chance meeting with her favorite actor and some nosy busy body had to ruin it." Then Aggie said, "I know! Especially since Alvin is in Europe doing who knows what with his tour mate. I don't want Malary to be crushed again. This could really push her over the top poor thing."

They got the hint and got Dylan to meet Malary in his trailer very quickly, in and out they said. She shouldn't be getting special treatment.

Malary had no idea what she was in for. She felt like her best friends were kidnapping her. They said just be quiet and use your ninja skills to get you in and out of this trailer as soon as possible. Malary was looking at them both and said, "Are you both drunk? ... What am I supposed to do in this trailer that's so important?" And with that Dylan Crane opened the door and said in his British accent, "I thought I heard voices. You must be Malary, come on in my lovely." Malary's knees went weak and she said, "Ok" as she glided into his trailer. Surprisingly to Malary the conversation was flowing with Dylan just as it had with Alvin but Dylan was more forward and said he was only supposed to give her a picture and an autograph but he was having so much fun he'd forgotten about that. And took her hand and asked if she could show him around the next day after his beach scene. He said "Just because we can't be seen on camera together doesn't mean we can't be together at all does it?" Malary blushed and said, "No, I guess it doesn't. But I do have a boyfriend so I just have to give him a heads up what's going on just in case." Dylan respected that and he kissed the top of her hand and said, "I'll see tomorrow Malary"

Chapter 10

The New Love

  Malary told Alvin about meeting Dylan and showing him around town for the movie. Alvin was understanding and said he had to sing a few love songs with Katherine Amanda Driscoll and people will probably think they're dating but they're not. He also said he couldn't call her for a couple of days because they had a lot of rehearsing to do and she's a real stickler for perfection. She understood and she trusted him completely. He said to have fun but not too much fun and she the same to him.

  The next day Malary filmed her scenes with Aggie and Niffer then waited for Dylan to finish his beach scene. It had taken longer than they had hoped because it was so hot and humid, they kept having to cool off in between takes. Dylan was sweating too much and also needed to hydrate. By the end of the day it was too late to really spend too much time with him. Dylan still wanted to see her though so they went on her parents boat she figured they could talk and laugh as much and as loud as they wanted without keeping anyone up and being in public. It had been during the week so Josie had Jaycee were home. Malary and Dylan were all alone on the boat.

The more they talked and hung out the more she was getting attracted to him and him to her. He wasn't just all muscle and blonde hair and piercing light blue eyes he was also really down to earth and super easy to talk to. He could laugh at himself and she loved that about him. But the more she was falling for Dylan the worse she felt about Alvin. How could she love him so much but feel something else for another man at the same time?

Alvin hadn't called Malary at all the next day. She was beginning to think she'd hurt him by hanging out with Dylan. So, she didn't call Dylan that day either. She figured some time by herself to think about everything was what she needed to do. Malary went to her cousin's house and decided to pool it for the rest of the day. Let the universe tell her what she should do. That night after dinner she was watching tv in her room. The news had showed pictures of Alvin with his tour mate in Paris getting cozy shopping around together and going out to eat around the riviera. Before she could even form a thought about what she had just seen she got a call from Dylan. "Hi there my lovely, did I do something wrong? I haven't heard from you all day. Is everything alright?" She said, "Hi Dylan. No, you didn't do anything I was just trying not to get too close to you because I didn't want to hurt Alvin. But it looks like he isn't worried about my feelings at all. Prancing all around Europe with his tour mate Katherine Amanda Driscoll. "Ugh!" Dylan said, "Katherine Amanda Driscoll? She's so high maintenance I don't think you have anything to worry about there. And I'm sorry if I'm coming on too strong. It's just that when I met you it was the first time I didn't feel so far away from my elements." She felt better about her and Dylan's friendship now. But the more she didn't hear from AJ the more she grew closer to Dylan. Two days turned into two weeks. When she saw a picture of Alvin with his arm around Katherine Amanda saying he's so lucky to have a great gal by his side being so far from home and his family it makes it a lot easier. Malary was pissed she called Dylan and they both looked at it together and she asked what he thought about it. He leaned into her and said, "I think this means I can kiss you now. Right?"

Chapter 11

The New Romance?

Malary gave into Dylan. That kiss was so amazing it could have literally knocked her socks off. It was so passionate and she felt her body's temperature rising from head to toe as he held her face to his. Dylan wanted to do everything with her from that moment on. Malary's parents didn't like that she just assumed Alvin had dumped her and moved on so quickly but Dylan was really charming and he was 10 years younger than Alvin so that helped.

Malary also blew off school so she could be with Dylan traveling and seeing the world. Dylan was the complete opposite of Alan. He could never sit still. He always had to be doing something or whisking her away on a whim. Dylan was never the type to have to have someone with him all the time. But he just loved her company and seeing the world through Malary's eyes.

Dylan never finished high school so he didn't get why an education was really necessary to succeed in life. He does wish that he could sit and write something but he was never good at writing and he can't sit still long enough to anyway. Malary figured it was only one year she'd have to go back for anyway so she didn't think it was that big of a deal. Dylan convinced her to spend a month in Maine to see the foliage and they rented a house by the beach.

It was too cold to be on or in the water. But Malary enjoyed their sunset walks on the beach. They would get pastries from Congdon's donuts in the morning and coffees at night and they'd just walk and talk. The night before Dylan had to leave for New York he asked Malary to go with him and he'd show her all around there. He had his own flat and he was going to start filming there soon too. Malary couldn't wait to spend more time getting to know Dylan. He was the perfect gentleman and so posh but still silly in his own way. It was hard to turn him down really. Looking at that chiseled jaw line and those dimples. Plus, he had a killer body. Then he asked if she was ready to spend the night with him, she immediately thought of Alvin and what he could be doing, she still hadn't heard from him in about two months now. Every time she called him it went to straight to voicemail and she had filled his voicemail up with all the messages she had already left him.

She figured no one would know except her and Dylan anyway so she agreed to sleep with him that night. She was really nervous only really being with Alvin and Dylan was so experienced she thought he'd change his mind if she told him that. So, she just tried to relax and enjoy everything about him. Maybe him being so experienced was a good thing. Her and Dylan found it hard to stop once they started. He knew exactly where to touch her and what to do to please her. When they eventually tired each other out. She fell asleep on him and he wrapped his arms around her and fell asleep too.

The next morning, she woke up and Dylan had already showered and dressed and styled his spiky blonde hair then got breakfast for her. She thought this is the life. He really did treat her like royalty. She couldn't wait to see what life in New York was like with him. She also was wondering about Aggie in Nashville in school by herself for the first time. She was going to have to go back to Nashville eventually. Her and Dylan made a pact. They'd spend two weeks in New York then two weeks in Nashville.

Life in New York was fast paced and hectic. Everyday there was an issue with the movie Dylan was in so he kept getting called to the set. Dylan had told Malary to go shopping or do something fun but that's not her style. She'd rather be on a boat or driving her truck or riding horses or playing her guitar, and she missed her parents and her dog Tiny. None of which was available for her in New York City. She barely even had time to spend with Dylan when he was in the apartment, he was either working on lines or at the set. Malary began to think this city really doesn't sleep because even when they think they're in for the night sometimes he has to take off again. She began to wonder if there was someone else but the other woman was showbiz. Dylan's holiday time was almost here though and they'd spend two wonderful weeks in the country. She couldn't wait to go back to Nashville and show off her beau!

It was a different feeling not having Alvin get her at the airport. Instead Dylan had got a limo to bring them to her and Aggie's place. Aggie was so happy Malary was back. She was a little disappointed she had Dylan with her but once his holiday was over, he'd leave for a few weeks then he'd come back or Malary would leave again. Aggie really missed having Alvin around then her best friend would stay and be her true self again. She liked Dylan Crane but not for her best friend.

In Nashville Dylan was just as miserable as Malary was in New York. After a few days of riding around and showing him the lake life with the fishing and the horses and the live music downtown he was really getting bored. He told Malary one night, "I'm sorry I can't take it here. I need to be doing something with my time. Something productive. Not riding around in jeeps and taking care of horses and fishing all day. This is torture for me!" Malary chimed back, "Torture? You want to know what torture is, it's being cooped up in an apartment all day and night with no friends, no backroads or beaches to get lost in, you can't even see the stars there and there aren't any lighting bugs to catch at night either." Dylan yelled back, "Well sorry I'm not the hick you fell in love with here! I guess we're just too different people who grew up on the two different sides of the pond!" Malary said, "I guess so. And Alvin's not a hick." Dylan said, "What did you just say?" Malary said, "Nothing." Dylan insisted, looking down at her with an angry look in his eyes, trying to intimidate her. He did look rather scary when he said, "What did you say?!" Malary was going to look away but she stood up to him instead and yelled at him. "ALVIN IS NOT A HICK!" With that Dylan grabbed his things and said, "I can see I'm not wanted here anymore. Goodbye and good luck with that HICK!" Malary was so furious. Aggie said, "I've never seen you so upset. You actually yelled. I didn't think you had it in you!... Well I'm glad he's gone. You weren't you with him around."

Chapter 12

The Comeback Kid

Malary took Aggie's words to heart. She knew she wasn't herself with Dylan. She was up and she was down, wondering what kind of mood he would be in after work. It was not a good situation always having to feel like she was walking egg shells around him not to upset him. Plus, she was always thinking about Alvin. She wondered why he hadn't tried to contact her at all this past year. Malary got a hold of his Mama just like she did when Alvin was in bad shape and needed her. Now she's in bad shape emotionally and mentally and needs Alvin. His Mama answered her phone. "This is Mama Jean; can I ask who is calling?" Malary said, "It's me, Mama Jean, it's Malary." Mama Jean was so elated! She said, "Why thank the heavens my prayers have been answered! I'll tell him you called. He's been tryin' to reach you but couldn't get through. He's been seeing that girl he's on tour with and he's miserable poor thing."

Malary called Alvin's hotel straight away, Alvin was out so she had left a message for him, "Hi Al this is Mal I miss you and I'm not me when I'm not with you so please call me back. Love you." She thought the cute nicknames would be endearing and hoped it made him want to call her back as soon as he got the message. She was eager to hear back from him and hoped they could pick up from where they had left off. She didn't know that she'd have to keep waiting. For two more weeks Malary waited. She waited by the phone. She waited at her and Aggie's house. She waited at his house (across from his driveway actually, there were gates at the entrance so she couldn't actually wait at his house) but she waited so long she was losing hope. She was about to call his Mama again but she learned his dad was ill and she knew she had to be there for Alvin.

   Malary tried every source she could think of trying to find out more information where Alvin could be. She thought of contacting his band members. She finally got up the nerve to go to Florida maybe he was there with his family and she'd show him how much she really cared.

   Malary found his parents' house. His sisters and brother in laws were staying there also so maybe they could help her find the hospital his dad was at. She was in luck one of his nephews was outside she explained who she was and she needed to find Alvin. He told her the hospital they were at and said his mother Kathy would be waiting for her outside to let her in. When she got there there were a lot of paparazzi so she wanted to make sure Malary got in without being seen. Kathy was there outside and she showed her in. She said Alvin was getting them coffees and would be back shortly if she wanted to wait. All his sisters were so happy and appreciative that she was there.

When she saw Alvin walk in, she got up from her seat to help him with the coffees then to hug him. He said, "I should be furious with you but I'm really glad to see you." This isn't the place or time to discuss what's going on with us," Malary said. "I'm just here to lend a hand or a shoulder." And with that Alvin took her hand and said, "This will do for now." And they grinned at each other and sat for a while. Alvin did mention that he was miserable in Europe and Katherine Amanda Driscoll. All she wanted to do was shop and eat at all these fancy places and go to the most elite parties. She was so high maintenance everything had to be to her standards even down to what he wore. He couldn't take it. He went in hiding after that for a while just so she wouldn't track him down. She had deleted every call and text message from Malary to Alvin also, so he had no idea she was trying to get in touch with him. That's why he didn't call, he thought she had moved on while he was on tour and he was only trying to do pass the time until he came back home. But then his dad suddenly got sick and he had to be by his side and with his family, so he came out of hiding. He told Malary, "I knew it from the very first smile. You never looked at me or treated me like a celebrity. That's how I knew I was in love with you. That will never change."

Chapter 13

The Fishing Trip

Alvin and Malary are in Florida. They've been staying on Alvin's boat there since his dad had passed and they wanted to be close to his Mama and sisters for a bit longer. Alvin had a small place close to his parents' house with a dock so he could stay on the boat while some family members stayed at his house. Valentine's Day was coming up and Alvin wanted to do something special for Malary. He knew she always wanted to go deep sea fishing with him in hopes of catching a marlin.

Alvin took her to dinner one night at a restaurant at his favorite Marina. They had chowder and swordfish and corn on the cop with baked potatoes. For dessert they went out for ice cream then headed back to the boat. Alvin told Malary to rest up because first thing in the morning at sunrise they were taking off. Malary said, "What? Where are we going? I don't have all my things here. How long are we going for?" Alvin chuckled and said, "No need to pack or bring anything special. If we decide to stay out longer or go anywhere else besides, oh I don't know fishing for blue marlins then we'll stop and you can get whatever you need and want on me!" Malary was so excited. She asked, "How did you know I want to go fishing for blue marlins anyway?" Alvin shrugged and said, "I heard it through the grapevine… and you also have a marlin tattoo with the notes from my song "Blue Marlin." Malary blushed and said, "Oh yea that's kinda obvious huh?" They both laughed and tried to get to some sleep. But Malary was so excited she could hardly sleep that night. Alvin could feel her tossing and turning so he spooned her and rubbed her neck and shoulder until she fell asleep.

Malary woke up to the smell of fresh coffee and Alvin was making pancakes and eggs before they took off at sun break. Malary said, "Why do fish only bite so early in the morning? Are they really that smart? Don't they know by now that we've caught on to them?" Alvin laughed and said, "You make absolutely no sense this early in the morning. Haha." She took a sip from her coffee and waited for Alvin to finish making their breakfast so they could start their fishing trip.

They took off out to the ocean Alvin's boat "Fish Magnet" was the only one out there. Malary sat by him with her cup of coffee close by to keep her up. They drove out for about 45 minutes then dropped anchor and Alvin set up the boat with the fishing gear in hopes Malary would catch her first marlin. He said, "These guys are pretty fast and hard to catch. But we'll stay out here until you catch one. Even if it takes all year!" Malary said, "Geez thanks for the boost of confidence." They both snickered and got ready to fish. About an hour and a half went by with no luck. Malary was starting to get hungry again so she had some ginger snaps and ginger ale. The boat was rocking a lot out in the wide-open seas so she was getting a little queasy at times. Alvin was really sweet and would move the boat around if she was feeling sick. They get some wind in their faces then go swimming. By night time he cooked the fish they did catch, not marlins though. After supper they'd go on the bow of the boat and lay and stare at the stars until Malary fell asleep in Alvin's arms and he'd carry her to bed.

It was almost the end of the week and they hadn't caught one marlin Malary was starting to lose hope and thought, even if they didn't catch one it was still a perfect get away. Malary felt Alvin get out of bed but she couldn't get the will power to get up herself just yet. Then Alvin came to wake her up. Alvin said, "Wake up honey! This sunrise is unbelievable you don't wanna miss it!" Malary got up and threw a blanket around herself. Alvin held her close while they watched the sunrise sipping their coffee and Malary dozed off again until Alvin woke her up for some breakfast sandwiches, he made, then time to catch her a marlin!

Usually marlins aren't common in this area or around this time of year but that didn't stop Alvin from trying for Malary. They caught mostly smaller fish mostly trout. Even though they didn't catch any marlin on this trip it was nice to spend time together just the two of them. By the time they got back to shore Alvin had to go back on tour and Malary would go home to her parents before spending some time with Aggie and Niffer. Before Alvin got back to Nashville Mal and Al felt their love for each other was stronger than ever now. He promised to call her every night before his shows and text her good night afterwards even if she was already sleeping. They weren't going to let anything come between them this time.

Chapter 14

The High School Sweetheart

When Alvin and Malary got back to his Mama's house in Jupiter they walked in to see how Mama Jean was doing. She was surrounded by family and to Alvin's surprise his high school sweetheart Jeanine Johnson. Jeanine was sitting by his mom when he walked through the door, she ran to him and screamed his name and threw her arms around him. Alvin was in such shock he didn't even know what to say or do. He stumbled on his words, "Jeanine what? Hi. What are you doing here? It's been years since I've seen you." Jeanine replied, "Yes it's been too long. I can't believe how time has flown by! I'm so sorry about Daddy Joseph." And she hugged him again. Mama Jean grabbed Malary's hand and lead her over to Alvin and said "Why don't you introduce Jeanine to your girlfriend who's been here all along and is just a joy, I don't know what this boy would have done without her!" Malary blushed but before she could say anything Alvin wrapped his arm around her and concurred, "Mama's right I would have been lost without her. She's been my rock." Jeanine leaned in to shake Malary's hand and said, "Well if you mean that much to AL then I need to get to know you better. Why don't we get together while AL's on tour?" Malary smiled and shook her head, "I can't, I need to go home to New England to be with my family for Easter. It's at my parents' house and I," Jeanine cut her off and turned to Alvin, "What are you gonna do without your rock by your side on the road?" Alvin curled his nostrils and said, "I know how important family is and she needs to see her parents and her family for the holidays. Besides it's none of your business what we do anyway. If you really came here because you care then act like it." Jeanine put her hands to her face, "Oh my, I'm so sorry you're right. I apologize if I came off too aggressive. I guess I still feel over protective of AL. I truly apologize. Let's start over. We need to get together when AL gets back or something." Malary thought more like territorial of ALVIN was more like it but what the heck, "Sure we will, definitely." Jeanine hugged them both and left. Alvin turned to Malary put his hands on her shoulders, rubbing her arms up and down saying, "I'm so so so so so so very sorry about that. I didn't know she'd be here. I didn't know she'd act like that. I hadn't seen her since I left college to move to Nashville." Malary grabbed Alvin's hands and pulled them to her chest under her chin," Alvin you don't need to apologize. I know you love me and you know I love you and that's all that matters."

   All the way back to her family all Malary could think about was how Alvin stood up to Jeanine like that. What a man. She was so proud to be with him. Malary finally felt like they were at a steady point in their relationship. She told Aggie and Niffer all about her trip with him and what happened with Jeanine. They were happy he stood up to her too and they couldn't wait to see him in concert at the end of April. Things were finally falling in place. Aggie was just happy to have her best friend back and Niffer was happy that both her best friends were happy and everything was going to get back to normal around here.

Chapter 15

The Old flames

With Alvin on tour for the next two weeks Malary went home to New England to be with her family. Aggie was home too because school was on spring break. They were also missing Niffer a lot so they planned on going to see her one weekend also. Alvin promised to call Malary at any chance he got. It was only two weeks then Alvin would meet her in New England for some boating with Malary and Josie and Jaycee.

Aggie and Malary spent a few days hanging out together. They'd go for long drives in the country and by the water with their dogs. They would get ice cream and go to the beach to swim with the dogs then walk back to the truck to dry off. Malary would drop her off at her parents' house then go back home to eat dinner with her parents. Malary and Josie spent some time shopping together and spending some quality mother and daughter time talking and hanging out. She also spent some time talking with Jaycee on the boat.

One-night Niffer called Malary, "Have you seen AJ's fan page lately?", she asked Mal. Malary replied with, "No I try not to because I'll drive myself crazy with jealousy over nothing." Niffer said, "Well you probably shouldn't start looking at it now. Sorry to bum you out but you should really see who he's with." Now Malary was starting to shake, what was the issue? Who is he with? Why would Niffer be so concerned? She finally found his fan page and found a post one fan saw of Alvin with his ex, Jeanine. She thought that's no biggie. Then there was another one from a different night at a different location. Now this is kinda weird. "Why wouldn't Alvin tell me Jeanine was visiting him?"

Meanwhile back in Nashville Aggie got a surprise visit. Aggie went back to get settled in before school starts back up again after the break. There was a knock on the door and when she opened it there stood Dylan looking dapper and sexier than ever. She just stood there for a second staring at his piercing blue eyes and muscles popping out of his almost too tight sweater. Aggie muttered, "Dylan!" Dylan said in his British accent, "Hi Aggie may I come in?" Aggie told him, "Malary isn't here she's in New England with her parents and Alvin." Dylan looked disappointed all of a sudden. "She's with him now huh?" Aggie said, "Yes they're together again. Do you want me to leave a message for her?" Dylan looked at her and she could see the sadness in his eyes. "No, I'll come back another time. I just wanted to apologize for the way I left things last time I was here. I haven't been able to forgive myself for the way I treated her. But please don't say anything to her I want it to surprise her myself." Aggie agreed and Dylan gave her a peck on her cheek thanking her and he left feeling defeated. Aggie didn't like the idea of keeping this from Malary but she didn't want to ruin that moment for her either. She just thought he'd better come back soon!

  Back at Malary's parents house Alvin showed up. They hugged and kissed and Malary playfully hit Alvin's arm saying, "Why didn't you tell me Jeanine went with you to a couple of shows?" Alvin rubbed his arm and laughed, "She wasn't with me she went to a couple of shows and bought meet and greets in hopes of catching up or something. How did you find out she was there anyway?" Malary said, "My friends are on your fan page and saw pictures." He said, "See those pages are nothing but trouble." Malary glared at him. Alvin finished with, "I'm sorry though. I should have told you so you didn't have to find out that way." Malary said, "I forgive you and yes just be honest with me so I know what's going on next time." Alvin agreed then they went boating for the weekend with Josie and Jaycee.

  The four of them met up with a few of Malary's parents' friends and they all rafted up together. In the morning Alvin and Jaycee would get breakfast and coffees for the girls and bring it back to the boat. Some days they'd eat breakfast on the island. Then they would all go walk up to Circuit Ave and go shopping. They'd eat lunch somewhere outside because of Tiny. Usually they would eat inside at Nancy's but if Tiny was with them they'd have to eat outside where dogs were allowed and Tiny being a Great Dane well, he's not easy to hide! After lunch they'd walk and shop some more. Then go back to the boats and all eat dinner together. Sometimes they'd rent trucks or jeeps and go driving on the sand dunes and on rainy days go to the glass blowing store and watch them make some pretty neat things out of glass. Or they'd just sit on the boats all day and talk and catch some sun or jump in the water to cool off. Alvin loved it there because for the most part no one treated him any differently than anyone else. Once in a while in town someone might recognize him and ask for an autograph or something then they'd be reminded that he's famous but then they just carry on like it was normal.

Chapter 16

The Drama

Alvin was about to the second leg of his tour. Malary wanted to stay in Nashville this time. Help Aggie with what would have been their senior year. Aggie asked her, "Do you miss going to school with me at all?" Malary replied, "Yea sometimes I do. I love being able to go here and there whenever I want but I do miss our classes together and studying together." Aggie said, "I miss that too. Sometimes I get lonely out here all by myself." Then she thought of that day Dylan came by but she didn't bring it up. Malary apologized and said, "I'm here now until you graduate then we can figure out what to do about this house." The house was pretty perfect. Overlooking the lake, it's tiny but big enough for two but that's it. It's a perfect summer place if they wanted to keep it and rent it out. Aggie didn't want to move really though she just wanted her best friend there more often.

While Aggie was in class and with Alvin away on tour this gave Malary sometime to explore around the area more than she had before. She'd go downtown to Broadway and watch some live music while she had lunch then she'd do some shopping for the house here and there. Grab some groceries or whatever else they needed then went back. During the week she'd help

Aggie with her homework if she could in any way then they'd make supper and watch tv until they fell asleep then start all over again. On the weekends they might go see an Opry show or do something fun downtown.

One day the girls were out heading to Memphis for a road trip to Graceland when Malary got a message from a friend who's in Alvin's fan club. The message said "you've got to see this woman she's talking about you and Alvin like you stole him away from her!" Malary rushed to the page and sure enough there she was Rudy McCormick she posted all four concert tickets she had she was going to follow Alvin's bus to all locations and get meet and greets so she could "win" him back. One caption under a picture of them from an old meet and greet said, "Here we were before he got distracted by young blood." Malary heard of a fan who made up stories trying to get closer to AJ she even said if she had to cozy up to the band members to get back to AJ she would or just tell AJ that in fact Malary had done that already in attempt to get to him. Malary couldn't believe someone she had never even met would do that to her just to get to her boyfriend and try to steal him from her. She thought it was kind of funny after a while. She completely trusts Alvin and they're at a good point in their relationship now she didn't want to tell him about this until after if it came up somehow.

A few days later she was curious about what Rudy was posting about the first concert she stalked Alvin to. But Rudy hadn't posted anything yet to Malary's surprise. Aggie was in class and Malary decided she was just going to hang around the house today. She went out on the dock and sat on a chair in the sun. Tanning and reading, when she got too hot, she jumped in the lake to cool off. She missed having Tiny there to swim with and use a floaty. As she was coming out of the water, she heard someone drive up. She made her way to the side of the house and heard a man's voice saying, "Hello!" She responded, "Yes hi! I'm here!" Then she came face to face with Dylan Crane.

"Dylan wow this is a surprise!" Dylan smiled a little anxiously and said, "A good surprise I hope!" Malary gave him a side pout and didn't say anything. "I'm so sorry for the way I behaved last time we were here and were together. I need to make it right again." Dylan said hoping for Malary to forgive him and hopefully start over. Malary took a deep breath and said, "You couldn't have called or wrote a letter or sent a text or something?" Dylan explained, "No I couldn't chance you hanging up on me or ignoring a text or letter. This way I know either way yes or no. Can you ever forgive me and give me a second chance?" He scrunched down a little so he was face to face with her, she was shorter than him but he's not as tall as AJ so it wasn't too bad. His hands were clasped liked he was praying for her forgiveness. Malary said, "You know I've never yelled at anyone before. I didn't really care for it. I sounded like a crazy person." Dylan said, "I know I'm so sorry. I mean I know I made you yell, not I know you sounded like a mad person because you could never sound mad. Please give me another chance to make it up to you." Malary figured she'd forgive him and let him in or else he probably wouldn't leave her alone until she did. She had to change out of her wet bathing suit and in dry clothes anyway. Dylan said, "You look lovely by the way. I completely understand if you want me gone by the time Alvin gets home too." Malary smirked and said, "He's on tour so he won't be back for another couple of weeks. Are you staying at a hotel or anything?" Dylan said, "Nope. I figured if you didn't want to see me, I'd fly back to New York and if you did then I'd make arrangements to stay somewhere." Malary said, "Well you can stay tonight but that's it tomorrow find a hotel if you plan on staying longer." Dylan agreed to her terms.

  When Aggie got home, she was shocked to see Dylan and Malary making supper together and said, "I guess she forgave you!" Malary gave her a confused look. "Wait you knew he was coming here to apologize?" Aggie said, "Well in a sense but didn't know exactly when he'd be back. He came to see you when you were in New England with your parents and Alvin. Sorry I didn't tell you but we thought this way would be better." Malary said, "Yea better for him. If I had time to think about it, I probably would have said no!" And the girls laughed then Dylan laughed in relief in she was joking. Hopefully.

Chapter 17

Foggy situation

  The next morning Dylan had gone for a run then came back to shower in hopes he could get breakfast cooked for the girls before they woke up. Malary got up while Dylan was showering. She decided to make breakfast sandwiches and coffee. When Dylan got out of the shower breakfast was already done. Malary giggled at his wild wet hair but secretly thought it was really sexy. Dylan ran the towel through his short spiky blonde hair then threw the towel in the hamper and sat down at the table next to Malary. He kissed her cheek and thanked her for breakfast and the coffee. Malary reminded him she's still with Alvin. Dylan smirked and said, "I hope you know I was just simply thanking you. I'm European it's what we do!" Malary said, "Ok just reminding you. I'm not going to cheat on him." Dylan looked at her seriously and said, "Ok."

  "So, I was thinking we could go out on the water today. Take the boat out and go swimming and cook out on the water what do you think?" Malary looked at him confused and said, "Where are we getting a boat from?" Dylan pointed to their dock outside, Malary went back out through the front door and saw the pontoon baat docked outside. "Where the hell did you get the pontoon boat?" Dylan said, "I looked up the best boat rentals on the lake and saw this. I have it for the weekend. They docked it while you were changing. Like it?" Malary shrugged and said, "I guess it looks like fun." Dylan said, "Let's wake Aggie up and get going." Malary went to wake Aggie up but she was already up, "I wanted to make sure it was safe to come out. I didn't know if you'd be at each other's lips or at your throats." Malary said, "Not yet. I don't know what he's trying to do or prove but it's freaking me out. I'm just trying to play nice. I told Alvin that Dylan is here. He's not too happy about it but he's glad he's leaving soon."

   The three of them got on the boat and Dylan was the captain. He drove the boat down the lake and the girls talked and told Dylan what they had done with Alvin on boat rides. Dylan was getting bored of all the AJ talk so he decided to anchor out and eat the lunch he had made. They had their sandwiches and chips then waited and tanned a bit before jumping in the water. Aggie did prefer Dylan's lunch over Alvin's. She doesn't care for fish and tells Alvin she's allergic to it and then they'd laugh about it.

   The girls started to really miss Alvin now. They asked if they could head back home. Dylan wanted to stay and watch the sunset. Malary said, "That's not a good idea. It's not a full moon. If we can't see the difference between the land and the water, we're gonna be in trouble." Dylan didn't like to be told what to do. He felt like she was making it look like he didn't know what he was doing. She said, "Driving a boat in real life is different than driving one in a movie." Malary really wanted to sleep in the comfort of her own home in her bed not in a pontoon boat in the middle of the lake. Dylan insisted, "We can watch the sunset then head back. We didn't drive for that long. How hard is it to drive back it's still light out for a bit after the sunset? We'll be fine. Don't worry so much." But the girls were worried. They had never been on the water in Nashville without Alvin there. And he always said don't drive back at night if it's not a full moon.

Dylan started to bring the anchor up as it got darker and darker after the sun had set. The girls didn't want to say anything to hurt his feeling and make him lash out at them. Malary texted Alvin what was going on and he said he could be there first thing in the morning. "Just tell Dylan not to drive too fast and keep your eyes on the water at all times." So that's what Malary did. Dylan said, "Once again, I know what I'm doing. I drove at about 35 knots for a half hour in this direction so that's what I'm doing on the way back." Aggie and Malary were so scared. It wasn't like they'd be lost at sea or anything but what if he hit something? It was dark now and he was driving so fast. Malary reminded him, "Watch out for other boats." Dylan ignored her. He started to get scared himself. He started to slow down and asked the girls, "Would you both feel better if we anchored out for the night?" The girls looked at each other than at him and Aggie said, "Well we'd really feel more comfortable if we knew where we were." Dylan scoffed and sped up again then he stopped and said, "I'm going to drop anchor and head back after sunrise."

The girls were so nervous about another boat hitting them and they were tired and hungry. It was getting chilly too and they didn't bring anything other than light jackets. The pontoon cushions weren't that comfortable to lay on. The girls couldn't help but think who knows who has sat on these cushions and if they had been washed recently?

   Malary and Aggie hardly slept. Dylan was snoring away and it was almost light out. The girls could hear a boat coming. The sound of the motor got louder and louder. They got on either sides of the boat and tried to see which direction it was coming from. Finally, they saw it coming and Malary blew the horn, waking Dylan up. He jumped up saying, "For F@&k sake! What the F$&k!?" Malary said "There's a boat heading right towards us I'm letting them know we're here." Dylan said, "We don't need saving I can get us back." The boat was turning all around during the night everything looked different now. He started up the boat and as he was about to lift the anchor the boat pulled up beside them. It was Alvin! He said, "Good morning ladies! Hey Mal, how I've missed you. Get on I'll bring you home. Dylan you can follow us back." Dylan didn't say a word to Alvin, he just followed them back. When they got to the dock at the house Alvin jumped off the boat and guided it in using the lines the girls threw to him off the bow and the port side, tying it off at the cleats. Dylan had a hard time docking the pontoon by himself so Alvin jumped on and threw a line to Malary which she put around a cleat and held it trying to guide him in behind Alvin's boat. Then he ran to the bow and threw a line to

Aggie and she did the same. Alvin looked over to Dylan and said, "This will go a lot smoother if I take the wheel." Dylan reluctantly let go of the wheel and got out of Alvin's way. Alvin and Dylan got on the dock, Alvin scolded him, "Don't come around here ever again. I never want to hear your name come out of my girls mouth again." Dylan went to grab his things and said, "Once a hick, always a hick." Under his breath.

Chapter 18

The Fan Drama

When everything settled down after Dylan left, Malary had the chance to ask Alvin about Rudy McCormick. "So, what's up with that stalker fan? I heard some lady followed your bus to like four of your shows and bought meet and greets for all four shows." Alvin looked confused with one eyebrow raised up and curved over his left eye. He said, "Yea... Uh how did you know about that?" Malary looked at him with a sly look in her eyes and said, "You know I've got connections." Aggie said, "Yup! Me and Niffer got her back you know that!" Alvin smiled and chuckled, "Baby you ain't got nuttin' to worry about. Your man is always prepared for crazed fans. My band and security are top notch." Malary chimed in, "Yes they are but she's going around saying I slept my way to you through your band when in fact she's been trying to do that. Like you said, your band members are too smart for that and they all know me and how I feel about all of you." Alvin said, "How do you feel about them?" With a twinkle in his eye. Malary said, "They're all a bunch of jerks!" And laughed, "They're all great. Even though they were concerned about us in the beginning. But that shows they've got your back. So, I can't hold that against them."

Alvin said, "We have special precautions for people like that. We put up barricades and have heightened security. Plus, since the band knows what they look like because they go out and talk to the fans and sign things while I'm getting ready to leave, they can pin point who they are for the next time they see them and they give me the heads up. It just isn't fair for those fans who are there for the music and want a good experience. I can't give my all when the barriers are there. It makes it difficult to sign things from the stage at the end of my shows. Especially when she hogs the stage with her posse and her whole wardrobe for me to sign." He says with an eye roll. The girls have heard about her through other fans they befriended over the years. Aggie didn't like her lying about her best friend, "I wish there were a way to get her to change her ways." Alvin said, "Sometimes there are things you can't control. We have just had to do the best we can not to get wrapped up in that. Unfortunately, I have to deal with things like this to do what I love."

"Hey speaking of concerts! I've got a great idea! I could put on a tour of just water concerts. Perform at marinas or lakes, anywhere where we can get tons of boats to anchor out and party." Malary and Aggie loved that idea. Malary called Jaycee right away and asked him to talk to the marina his boat was at and tell them his friend Alvin Jasper wanted to do a concert there and they'd be getting a call from his manager to go over the details. Alvin smirked and said, "Let's see people like Ruby try to ruin this type of venue."

Alvin performed anywhere he could from the ocean to the lakes and any marina he could get enough boats in. The concerts went from California to Massachusetts. It ended at the marina Malary's parents had their boat docked at. Malary was so excited she was going to be able to show off her man to her marina family. Not all of them had the pleasure of seeing Alvin in concert so this was the perfect opportunity. Malary, Aggie, and Niffer stayed on Jaycee and Josie's boat to watch the show. They also invited some friends from the fan club that didn't have boats.

Alvin performed his usual set plus some songs that were specifically about boating and some covers so that new fans could sing along to some songs too. Alvin had special guests come out to sing songs as well. He saved Malary's favorite song for last, "Blue Marlin." It was the best show Malary had ever seen.

After the show Alvin made his way to Jaycee and Josie's boat. He signed whatever people wanted him to and took pictures with everyone who wanted one with him. Josie kept the coffees coming for Alvin until he couldn't take it anymore. The show was on a Friday night so this way he could spend the weekend in New England with everyone. Jaycee said that was the best concert of his he's ever been to he didn't even fall asleep half way through! That had been a running joke since Malary was a teen and her parents took her, Aggie and Niffer to all his shows. Jaycee would fall asleep until Alvin did a cover song he recognized. He could fall asleep anywhere and, in any position, it was quite funny they all thought.

Alvin stayed at the marina all weekend to hang out with everyone. The marina family loved him and he loved them too, he fit right in with everyone there. He promised he'd be back and he couldn't wait for the next boating trip with everyone.

At the end of the weekend Malary and Alvin got ready to head back to Nashville. They loaded everything up in Malary's truck. This time they were going to drive back. Take their time and spend quality time together and they could bring Tiny with them. After the truck was loaded up Alvin wanted to walk down to the trees by the water. It was at the edge of the grass where the rocks met the ocean. There was a tree there that Malary would climb as a kid and walk dogs to, it was just so peaceful there and they would just sit there and watch the boats come in or just look at the water. Alvin wanted to take in as much as he could out of this weekend. He had such a great show and run of concerts that summer. They got to the tree and Alvin looked at Malary. He brushed the hair away from her face and tucked it behind her ear. He leaned in for a long passionate kiss then he got down on one knee. He took her left hand and said, "Malary you have made me so happy these past few years. I know we've had our ups and downs but I wouldn't want to have been through everything we've been through with anyone else. Will you marry me?"

Stay tuned for book two "Catching Blue Marlin" by Kirby Neto

If you enjoyed this story be sure to follow the Facebook page for Cowboy Daze for updates and some fun content.

www.ingramcontent.com/pod-product-compliance
Lightning Source LLC
Chambersburg PA
CBHW020958090426
42736CB00010B/1368